Wedding Bouquets

Mary Gudgeon & John Clowes

M & J PUBLICATIONS

CONTENTS

INTRODUCTION 3

BEFORE YOU START
Choosing materials for the dresses 4
Deciding flower types & colours 5
The mechanics 6-7

BOUQUETS & DECORATIONS
Bridal bouquets 8-56
Head-dresses 57
Bridesmaids' flowers 58-61
Buttonholes and Corsages 62
Cake Tops 63-64

MAKING BOUQUETS & DECORATIONS
Glossary of terms 65
The shapes of bouquets 66-67
Wiring flowers and foliage 68-71
Making up sprays 72

STEP-BY-STEP INSTRUCTIONS
Before you start 73
Shower Bouquet 74-76
Waterfall Bouquet 77-78
Cake Top 79
Crescent Bouquet 80-81
Straight Bouquet 82-83
Loose Posy 84-85
Posy Using Foam-Topped Handle 86
Victorian Posy 87
Pomander 88-89
Head-dresses 90
Buttonholes and Corsages 91
Ribbons and Ribboned Handles 92-95

INDEX 96

First published in Great Britain in 1987 by M & J Publications, The Hollies, Cattlegate Road, Crews Hill, Enfield, Middx, England EN2 9DW. (0992) 461895
Reprinted 1988

ISBN 0 9509748 2 X

Bouquets by Mary Gudgeon – © Copyright John Clowes 1987
Production Services by Book Production Consultants, Cambridge.
Printed in Great Britain by Butler & Tanner Ltd, Frome and London
Materials by Just Fabrics, Enfield 01-363-1690
Photography by Carleton Photographic Services Ltd (0992) 27866
Artwork and design by Broxbourne Design (0992) 441726

OTHER TITLES IN THE SERIES
'Silk Arrangements' shows how anyone can create beautiful permanent flower arrangements for the home using artificial blooms and foliage. Full page pictures of 32 arrangements together with detailed shopping list for each with step-by-step instructions and illustrations for easy assembly. All the designs are also suitable for use with fresh flowers. 96 pages.

'Christmas Arrangements' shows in a similar way how to create delightful decorations for the festive season. It is full of colourful arrangements which will add sparkle, excitement and your own touch of luxury to the Christmas festivities. 96 pages.

Available from garden centres, book shops or can be ordered direct from M & J Publications – Telephone (0992) 461895 for details of current costs.

Introduction

Traditionally, flowers play a vital role in the celebration of a wedding. The bride and her attendants will be the centre of the floral decorations, although the locations for the ceremony and reception will also be blessed with their fair share.

As the focal point of everyone's attention, the bride will need to plan her dress and flowers with care and precision. Many brides will rely on a qualified florist to create her bouquet and arrange the flowers for the bridesmaids, guests and the reception tables. Others will have a friend or relation who would like to take over all or part of this job.

With this exciting and colourful book you will find many ideas for colours and shapes of bridal bouquets and bridesmaids' flowers. Those people with do-it-yourself plans will also find advice on how to prepare both silk and fresh flowers and step-by-step instructions on how to make bouquets of all shapes and designs.

Although bouquets are not the easiest of things to create, the instructions found at the back of the book will simplify the process. With a little practice anyone with some knowledge will be able to adapt and create their own ideas for wedding bouquets and decorations. The bouquets in this book have been created using silk material so as to ease the problems of economical photography. They can all be made with fresh flowers.

Choosing materials for the dresses

Flowers play a secondary part to the dresses of the bride and bridesmaids. It is important, therefore, that the styles and materials for the dresses should be decided before you think of the flowers.

Whether buying ready-made, hiring or having made to order you should select the material and colour first so that the flowers can complement the dresses.

We have shown on this page just a few of the materials which are currently available. A specialist supplier will be able to show you hundreds of samples so that you can find the best that you can afford.

The materials used in this book were supplied by Just Fabrics, 4 Southbury Road, Enfield Town, Middx. EN1 1YT, Telephone 01-363-1690, who we would like to thank for their help.

Flower types and colours

Traditionally white is the colour for bridal flowers. Symbolising purity, most bouquets for the bride will contain some white blooms and there are plenty to choose from. Orange blossom, roses, stephanotis, lilies, freesias, marguerites, carnations and Lily of the Valley are most often used. Not to be forgotten are the more exotic white flowers of gardenias, orchids, camellias, azaleas, chincherinchee, carnations and myrtle.

The latter has been included in many Royal bouquets in the last few centuries. A piece of myrtle from Queen Victoria's bouquet was planted by her in Cowes on the Isle of Wight and it has been included in all the recent Royal wedding bouquets.

Nowadays there are no rules or conventions which dictate which flowers are acceptable for a bridal bouquet – almost anything goes. Of course the size of the bouquet and the shape selected will influence the most appropriate flowers. If you are using fresh flowers, the season will also influence the choice. With silk flowers you can ignore the time of year and select whatever you fancy.

If white is not to be the dominant colour then most brides prefer a pastel shade for the bouquet and usually choose something which will tone in with the bridesmaids' dresses. The determining factor as to colour and shape should however, be that the bouquet complements the dress of the bride.

The equipment and mechanics you will need

For Bouquets and Corsages

1. Wire
All silk and fresh flowers for inclusion in a bouquet will need to be wired individually. This enables the blooms to be made into groups or 'sprays' or subsequently to be positioned in the bouquet.

Reels of silver rose wire and packets of stub wire are available in various lengths and thicknesses. The finest wire is used for tiny flowers and for making sprays. Here are details of some of the most commonly used wires for bouquet work:-

Thin silver wire	36 gauge (0.22mm)	Choose one of these
	34 gauge (0.24mm)	
Medium wire	32 gauge (0.28mm)	Choose one of these
	28 gauge (0.38mm)	
Stub wire	26 gauge (0.46mm)	Essential
Stub wire	22 gauge (0.71mm)	Essential

2. Wire Cutters
Florist scissors often have a special notch which is suitable for cutting thin wire although these wire cutters, specially produced for floristry work, are better.

3. Scissors
For trimming foliage and cutting ribbons.

4. Stem-wrap or Florist's Tape
For covering the wire stems to give a natural green colour or white. Also used for binding the stems of individual flowers or sprays together to form the bouquet.

5. Pearl Headed Pins
Used to hold ribbon in place when used to cover a handle.

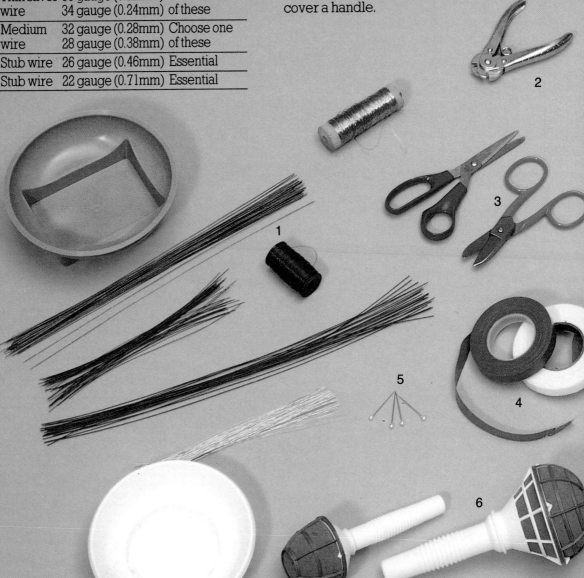

6. Foam-Topped Handles
Ideal for making posies and available in white.

7. Posy Frills

For Cake Tops

8. 'Stay Soft' or Dri-Hard
This type of material can be wrapped in aluminium foil and pushed into a decorative vase. Dri-Hard sets solid in a couple of hours. Wired flower stems pushed into this material will then remain in position.

9. Decorative Cake Vases

For Baskets and Pomanders

10. Plastic Foam
Use the green type for fresh flowers which will support the natural stems and supply moisture for continued freshness. Use the brown type either in block form or ball shapes to hold wired stems.

11. Plasticine Anchors
This tiny four-pronged anchor is used to hold foam in the basket or container. The anchor is stuck to the base of the container with Oasis fix. With large blocks use more than one anchor.

12. Oasis Fix
This fixative material is used to secure the plasticine anchor to the base of the container. Oasis fix is a brand name for one of these fixatives, but others are just as suitable.

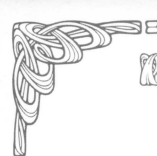

Style – Shower

Ingredients

Ivy Leaves
  4 stems x 3 leaves
  2 stems x 2 leaves
Gypsophila
  3 stems x bunches of florets
Lily of the Valley
  8 stems x 1 flower spike of various
  lengths
White Rose
  3 stems x 2 buds
  1 stem x 3 buds
  3 stems x full flower
White Freesia
  4 stems

White Stephanotis
  1 stem x 4 flowers
  5 stems x 3 flowers
  1 stem x 2 flowers
White Marguerite
  4 stems x 2 flowers
  1 stem x 1 flower
White Azalea
  3 stems x 2 flowers
White Lace Ribbon
  1 yard (1m) x 1½" (4cm) wide for
  double tails
  2 yards (2m) x ¾" (2cm) wide for
  handle
Pearl Headed Pins x 2

Length 19" (49 cm)
Width 10" (25 cm)

LEMON LILIES

Style – Shower

Ingredients

Lily
    3 stems x 1 full flower
    1 stem x 3 buds
    1 stem x 1 bud
Chrysanthemum
    2 stems x 3 flowers
    2 stems x 2 flowers
    1 stem x 5 buds
    1 stem x 4 buds
    1 stem x 2 buds

Carnation
    1 stem x 3 flowers
    1 stem x 2 flowers
    1 stem x 1 flower
White Satin Ribbon
    1 yard (1 m) x ¾″ (2 cm) wide for centre bow
    3 yards (3 m) x ¾″ (2 cm) for handle and double tails
Pearl Headed Pins x 2

Length 21″ (54 cm)
Width 9″ (23 cm)

SHADES OF PINK

Style – Shower

Ingredients

Dark Pink Carnation
8 stems x 1 flower
Medium Pink Lily
4 stems x 2 flowers
1 stem x 2 buds
Lily of the Valley
1 stem x 3 spikes
4 stems x 2 spikes
11 stems x 1 spike
White Freesia
8 stems x 1 flower
White Gypsophila
11 stems x 2 bunches

Pale Pink Chrysanthemum
8 stems x 1 flower including buds
Medium Pink Rose
9 stems x 1 flower
Lily Leaves
4 stems x 1 leaf
Pink Satin Ribbon
3 yards (3m) x ¾" (2cm) wide for handle
Pearl Headed Pins x 2

Length 20″ (50cm)
Width 11″ (28cm)

RED & WHITE CRESCENT

Style – Crescent

Ingredients

Ivy Leaves
2 stems x 5 leaves
2 stems x 4 leaves
White Gypsophila
7 stems x 2 bunches
10 stems x 1 large flower spike
White Wild Rose
3 stems x 3 flowers
2 stems x 2 flowers
White Rose
6 stems x 1 bud

Red Rose
4 stems x 1 flower
2 stems x 2 buds
2 stems x 1 bud
Rose Leaves
2 stems x 3 leaves
White Satin Ribbon
3 yards (3 m) x ¾" (2 cm) wide for handle
Pearl Headed Pins x 2

Length 15″ (38 cm)
Width 14″ (35 cm)

BLUE & WHITE SEMI-CRESCENT

Style – Semi-Crescent

Ingredients

Blue Lily
3 stems x 3 flowers
1 stem x 2 flowers
White Wild Rose
1 stem x 4 flowers
3 stems x 3 flowers
White Stephanotis
2 stems x 4 flowers
2 stems x 3 flowers
Blue Single Daisy
2 stems x 4 flowers
4 stems x 3 flowers

Lily of the Valley
1 stem x 3 flower spikes
4 stems x 2 flower spikes
2 stems x 1 flower spike
Blue Rose
4 stems x 1 flower
Blue Rose Bud
1 stem x 2 buds
White Satin Ribbon
*2 yards (2m) x ½" (1cm) wide for
handle*
Pearl Headed Pins x 2

Length 18″ (46cm)
Width 10″ (25cm)

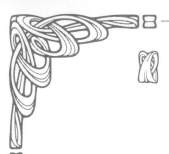

Style – Shower

Ingredients

Pink Orchid
  5 stems x 1 flower
Dark Pink Rose Buds
  3 stems x 2 buds
Pale Pink Rose
  4 stems x 3 roses incl. buds
  4 stems x 2 roses
Large Pale Pink Rose
  2 stems x 1 flower
Pale Pink Larkspur
  6 stems x 1 spike in various lengths
Small Medium Pink Daisy
  4 stems x 2 sprays

Large Medium Pink Daisy
  5 stems x 3 blooms
White Lily of the Valley
  7 stems x 2 spikes
Stephanotis
  2 stems x 4 flowers
  6 stems x 3 flowers
Croton Leaves
  3 stems x 1 leaf
Rose Leaves
  2 stems x 3 leaves
White Satin Ribbon
  2 ½ yards (2 ½ m) x ½″ (1 cm) wide for handle
Pearl Headed Pins x 2

Length 21″ (53 cm)
Width 13″ (33 cm)

LEMON & WHITE S

Style – S-Shaped

Ingredients

White Gardenia
4 stems x 1 flower
Yellow Lily
4 stems x 1 flower
1 stem x 1 bud
Yellow Rose
8 stems x 1 full flower
10 stems x 1 bud

Lily of the Valley
32 stems x 3 flower spikes
White Satin Ribbon
*2 yards (2 m) x ½" (1 cm) wide for
handle*
Pearl Headed Pins x 2

Length 24" (61 cm)
Width 10" (25 cm)

PEACH ROSES

Style – Shower

Ingredients
Peach Rose
  4 stems x 1 full flower
  11 stems x 1 bud
Rose Leaves
  12 stems x 3 leaves
Lily of the Valley
  27 stems of various lengths
White Lace Ribbon
  3 yards (3m) x ¾" (2cm) wide for
  handle
Pearl Headed Pins x 2

Length 18" (45cm)
Width 11" (28cm)

PINK & LEMON HANDSPRAY

Style – Shower

Ingredients
Pink Rose Buds
12 stems x 1 bud
Lemon Rose Buds
11 stems x 1 bud
Lemon Daisy
3 stems x 3 flowers
3 stems x 2 flowers
3 stems x 1 flower
Pink Gypsophila
3 stems x 2 bunches
11 stems x 1 bunch
Pink Satin Ribbon
2 yards (2 m) x ¾" (2 cm) wide for
handle
Pearl Headed Pins x 2

Length 13" (33 cm)
Width 7" (17 cm)

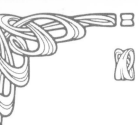

PEACH CASCADE

Style – Shower

Ingredients

Ivy Leaves
  2 stems x 11 leaves
  5 stems x 7 leaves
  1 stem x 5 leaves
Peach Rose
  4 stems x 3 flowers
  2 stems x 2 flowers
  2 stems x 1 flower
Peach Carnation
  1 stem x 4 flowers incl. bud
  6 stems x 4 flowers incl. bud
  2 stems x 3 flowers
Lemon Orchid
  4 stems x 1 flower
Peach Camellia
  4 stems x 1 flower
White Camellia
  2 stems x 3 flowers
White Freesia
  10 stems

Gold Alstroemeria
  2 stems x 5 flowers
  3 stems x 3 flowers
Lemon Delphinium
  2 stems x 7 florets
  1 stem x 5 florets
White Rose
  4 stems x 3 flowers incl. bud
  1 stem x 1 flower
Stephanotis
  1 stem x 13 flowers
  3 stems x 9 flowers
  2 stems x 8 flowers
  3 stems x 7 flowers
  3 stems x 6 flowers
  6 stems x 5 flowers
White Satin Ribbon
  4 yards (4 m) x 1" (25 mm) wide for handle
Pearl Headed Pins x 2

Length 33" (84 cm)
Width 20" (50 cm)

PEACHES & CREAM STRAIGHT BOUQUET

Style – Straight

Ingredients

Peach Rose
9 stems x 1 flower

Cream Orchid
9 stems x 1 orchid

Peach Lily
4 stems x 1 flower
5 stems x 1 bud and 1 flower

Peach Azalea
3 stems x 2 flowers
3 stems x 1 flower

Rose Leaves
14 stems x 3 leaves

Ivy Leaves
1 stem x 6 leaves
2 stems x 4 leaves
2 stems x 3 leaves

Cream Satin Ribbon
2 yards (2m) x ½" (1cm) wide for handle

Pearl Headed Pins x 2

Length 27" (69 cm)
Width 11" (28 cm)

29

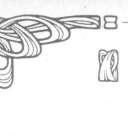

LEMON POSY

Style – Loose Posy

Ingredients
Lemon Rose
14 stems x 1 flower
Lemon Lily
17 stems x 1 flower
Lily Buds
7 stems x 1 flower
Rose Leaves
6 stems x 3 leaves
Ribbon Bows
9 x Double Loop Bows
Lemon Satin Ribbon
3 yards (3m) x ¼″ (5mm) wide for bows
2 yards (2m) x ½″ (1cm) wide for handle
Doily
Posy handle topped with
foam

Size 10″ (25cm) diameter

LARGE LEMON ORCHIDS

Style – Shower

Ingredients

White Agapanthus
2 stems x 5 florets
2 stems x 4 florets
1 stem x 3 florets
Lily of the Valley
5 stems x 1 long flower spike
White Stephanotis
1 stem x 5 flowers
2 stems x 4 flowers
1 stem x 3 flowers
Lemon Orchid
1 stem x 4 flowers
1 stem x 3 flowers
1 stem x 2 flowers
5 stems x 1 flower

Lemon Delphinium
1 stem x 7 florets
2 stems x 5 florets
1 stem x 4 florets
Yellow Lily
1 stem x 5 flowers
4 stems x 4 flowers
1 stem x 3 flowers
1 stem x 2 flowers
White Satin Ribbon
1 yard (1 m) x ¾" (2 cm) wide for centre bow
2 yards (2 m) x ½" (1 cm) wide for handle
Pearl Headed Pins x 2

Length 27" (69 cm)
Width 13" (33 cm)

APRICOT WATERFALL

Style – Waterfall

Ingredients

Apricot Rose
  7 stems x 1 rose
White Stephanotis
  1 stem x 7 flowers
  1 stem x 6 flowers
  1 stem x 5 flowers
  1 stem x 4 flowers
  2 stems x 3 flowers
Lily of the Valley
  9 stems of various lengths
Apricot Daisy
  3 stems x 5 flowers
  2 stems x 3 flowers

Cream Lily
  1 stem x 3 flowers
  2 stems x 2 flowers
  4 stems x 1 flower
Ivy Leaves
  1 stem x 9 leaves
  3 stems x 3 leaves
  1 stem x 1 leaf
Rose Leaves
  4 stems x 2 leaves
Peach Satin Ribbon
  *2 yards (2m) x ½″ (1cm) wide for
  handle*
Pearl Headed Pins x 2

Length 24″ (61 cm)
Width 12″ (30 cm)

SHADES OF LAVENDER

Style – Crescent

Ingredients

Pale Lavender Lily
  5 stems x 3 flowers
Medium Lavender Lily
  2 stems x 3 flowers
  2 stems x 2 flowers
  2 stems x 1 flower
Dark Lavender Lily
  1 stem x 3 flowers
  2 stems x 1 flower
Lavender Daisy
  4 stems x 3 flowers
  3 stems x 2 flowers

Rose Buds
  2 stems x 6 buds
  2 stems x 3 buds
Lavender Larkspur
  8 stems of various lengths
Ribbon Bows
  Double Loop Bows x 5
Lavender Satin Ribbon
  *3 yards (3m) x ½" (1cm) wide for
  double loop bows above*
  *2 yards (2m) x ½" (1cm) wide for
  handle*
Pearl Headed Pins x 2

Length 14" (35 cm)
Width 14" (35 cm)

PEACH LILIES & NET

Style – Semi Crescent

Ingredients

Peach Lily
    3 stems x 1 flower
    2 stems x 1 bud
Peach Rose
    6 stems x 1 flower
    1 stem x 5 buds
    1 stem x 4 buds
    1 stems x 3 buds
    1 stem x 2 buds
Lily Leaves
    5 stems x 1 leaf

White Daisy
    1 stem x 5 flowers
    1 stem x 4 flowers
    4 stems x 3 flowers
White Net
    2 yards (2 m) x 2" (5 cm) wide
    netting to make
    2 bows and 2 double tails
Peach Satin Ribbon
    2 yards (2 m) x ½" (1 cm) wide for
    handle
Pearl Headed Pins x 2

Length 16" (40 cm)
Width 10" (25 cm)

WHITE & LEMON SHOWER

Style – Shower

Ingredients

Gypsophila
9 stems x 1 spike of various lengths
Lily of the Valley
11 stems x 1 spike of various lengths
White Stephanotis
5 stems x 3 flowers
White Rose Buds
2 stems x 1 bud
Large White Rose
4 stems x 1 flower

Yellow Freesias
5 stems x 1 flower
4 stems x 1 bud and flower tip
White Orchid
3 stems x 1 flower
Asparagus Fern
12 stems x Fern
White Satin Ribbon
2 yards (2m) x ½″ (1cm) wide for handle
Pearl Headed Pins x 2

Length 23″ (59 cm)
Width 12″ (30 cm)

PEACH PIGTAILS

Style – Shower

Ingredients

Peach Orchid
  2 stems x 1 full flower
  1 stem x 1 bud
White Agapanthus
  2 stems x 5 florets
  4 stems x 3 florets
Peach Bell Flower
  1 stem x 3 flowers
  5 stems x 2 flowers
  3 stems x 1 flower

Peach Twirls
  2 stems x 3 twirls
Peach Pigtail Flower
  2 stems x 1 flower
White Satin Ribbon
  2 yards (2 m) x ¾" (2 cm) wide for handle
Pearl Headed Pins x 2

Length 24″ (61 cm)
Width 11″ (28 cm)

LEMON & PINK LOOSE POSY

Style – Loose Posy

Ingredients
Pink Rose
  9 stems x 1 flower
White Freesia
  8 stems x 1 flower
Lemon Wild Rose
  7 stems x 3 flowers
Rose Leaves
  8 stems x 3 leaves
Pink Satin Ribbon
  *2 yards (2 m) x ¾" (2 cm) wide for
  handle*
Pearl Headed Pins x 2

Size 11" (28 cm) Diameter

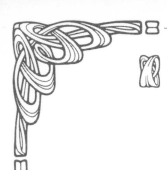

Style – Shower

Ingredients

Pink Lily
   1 stem x 3 buds
   1 stem x 2 flowers incl. 1 bud
   2 stems x 2 flowers
   3 stems x 1 flower
White Stephanotis
   1 stem x 5 flowers
   3 stems x 4 flowers
   4 stems x 3 flowers
Light Pink Rose
   4 stems x 3 flowers
   1 stem x 2 flowers

Marguerite
   2 stems x 4 flowers
   3 stems x 3 flowers
   2 stems x 2 flowers
   5 stems x 1 flower
Lily Leaves
   2 stems x 3 leaves
   2 stems x 2 leaves
White Satin Ribbon
   3 yards (3m) x ¾" (2cm)
   wide
Pearl Headed Pins x 2

Length 24" (60 cm)
Width 12" (30 cm)

LEMON & GREEN

Style – Straight

Ingredients

Lemon Carnation
  3 stems x 1 flower
Lemon Larkspur
  *8 stems x 1 spike of various
  lengths*
Lemon Azalea
  *2 stems x 3 flowers
  3 stems x 2 flowers*

Nephrolepsis (Fern) Leaves
  6 stems x 1 leaf
Lemon Satin Ribbon
  *2 yards (2m) x ½" (1cm)
  wide for double tails and bow
  loops
  2 yards (2m) x ½" (1cm)
  wide for handle*
Pearl Headed Pins x 2

Length 24″ (60 cm)
Width 7″ (12 cm)

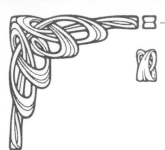

RED ROSES

Style – Shower

Ingredients

Red Rose
  2 stems x 2 roses
  9 stems x 1 rose
Rose Leaves
  9 stems x 3 leaves
Ivy Leaves
  3 stems x 3 leaves
  3 stems x 2 leaves
  1 stem x 1 leaf
White Agapanthus Florets
  1 stem x 5 florets
  6 stems x 4 florets
  10 stems x 3 florets

Lily of the Valley
  10 stems x 3 spikes
  2 stems x 4 spikes
  1 stem x 2 spikes
White Satin Ribbon
  2 yards (2m) x ½" (1cm)
  wide for handle and bow
  1½ yards (1½m) x ½" (1cm)
  if ribbon tails are required
Pearl Headed Pins x 2

Length 24" (60 cm)
Width 13" (32 cm)

OPEN PEACH POSY

Style – Loose Posy

Ingredients
Peach Orchid
 1 stem x 1 flower
Peach Rose
 3 stems x 2 flowers
White Freesia
 5 stems x 11 flower
Lemon Delphinium
 5 stems x 4 florets
Peach Lily
 3 stems x 1 flower
Marguerite Leaves
 10 stems x 1 leaf
Peach Ribbon Bows
 9 x Triple Loop bows
Peach Ribbon
 3 yards (3m) x ¼" (5mm)
 wide ribbon for Triple Loop bows
 2 yards (2m) x ½" (1cm)
 wide ribbon for handle and bow

Size 11" (28 cm) diameter

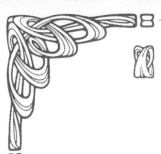

FREESIAS & PINK ROSES

Style – Shower

Ingredients
Pink Rose
10 stems x 1 flower
Roses should vary in shade and size
from buds to full rose.
White Freesia
11 stems
Pink Daisy
11 stems x 3 flowers
Gypsophila
18 stems x 5 flowers
This flower can be bought with
different sized blooms. The larger
type was used in this bouquet.
Pink Satin Ribbon
*2 yards (2m) x ½″ (1cm)
wide*
Pearl Headed Pins x 2

Length 14″ (35cm)
Width 10″ (25cm)

PEARL POSY

Style – Loose Posy

Ingredients
Pink Rose
18 stems x 1 bud
Pearl Heads
8 stems x 6 pearl flowers
Pink Daisy with Pearl Stamens
12 stems x 4 flowers
Pink Net Leaves
6 stems x 1 leaf
Posy Frill x 1
White Lace Ribbon
3 yards (3m) x ¾″
(2 cm) wide

Size 9″ (23 cm) diameter
Right of photograph

VICTORIAN POSY

Style – Victorian Posy

Ingredients
Dark Pink Rose
6 stems x 1 bud
Medium Pink Carnation
13 stems x 1 flower
Dark Pink Double Daisy
23 stems x 1 flower
Posy Frill x 1
Pink Satin Ribbon
3 yards (3 m) x ¼″ (5mm)
wide ribbon for trails
1 ½ yards (1 ½ m) x ½″ (1 cm)
for handle

Size 8″ (20 cm) diameter
Left of photograph

PINK BASKET

Style – Basket

Ingredients

Deep Pink Rose
11 stems x 1 flower
Pink Daisy
16 stems x 1 flower
White Rose
10 x 1 flower
White Gypsophila
21 x small bunch

Rose Leaves
15 stems x 3 leaves
Ribbon Bows
7 x Double Loop Bows
Dark Pink Ribbon
2½ yards (2½ m) x ½"
(1 cm) wide for bows above
1½ yards (1½ m) x ½" (1 cm)
wide for trail

Size 8" (20 cm) diameter

APRICOT POMANDER

Style – Pomander

Ingredients

Apricot Rose
9 stems x 1 flower
White Spiraea
20 stems x 1 flower (no leaves)
Apricot Azalea
11 stems x 1 flower
White Gypsophila
40 stems x 6 pieces

Foam Ball x 1
Ribbon Bows
16 x Double Loop Bows
2 x Triple Loop Bows
Apricot Satin Ribbon
8 yards (8m) x ½″ (1cm)
wide for bows above and handle

Size 8″ (20 x cm) diameter

Glossary of floristry terms

Binding – This is the term used for holding the material together when making a bouquet or corsage. It applies to binding with silver reel wire or with stem-wrap, Floratape or guttapercha. See pages 74-91.

Bouquet – An arrangement for a bride to carry. See next page for standard shapes.

Buttonhole – Worn by the groom, best-man, ushers and guests. See page 91.

Corsage – A small arrangement of several flowers worn on front of shoulder by special lady guests. Generally a very small bouquet. See page 91.

Double Leg Mount – This term is used when a wire is attached to short stem leaving 2 legs of wire same length. See pages 69 and 71.

Grouping – Flowers of one colour are placed together or run through a bouquet.

Guttapercha – Tape for covering a stem or wire and for binding.

Hairpin – Bending a wire to make double leg mount. See Page 68.

Pipping – Removing single florets from a flower and wiring individually. Often used with hyacinths and Lily of the Valley.

Feathering – Using small bunches of petals taken from one flower. Carnations are commonly used in this way. See Page 69.

Posy – Generally a round arrangement usually carried by bridesmaids.

Posy Frill – A doily, net or piece of lace which is used as a backing surround for posies.

Return End – When widest point of bouquet is reached and flowers are placed in for top of bouquet.

Single Leg Mount – This term is used when a wire is attached to short stem leaving one leg of wire. See page 69.

Sprays – More than one flower bound together with stem-wrap before commencement of bouquet making. See page 72.

Stem-wrap – Self-adhesive tape usually in white or green used to cover wires and to bind stems together.

Stitching leaves – Attaching a silver wire to the back of a leaf to give it stability. See page 70.

Taping – Using guttapercha or stem-wrap to cover wired stem or for binding sprays together to make a bouquet or corsage. See page 72.

Wiring – Making false stems when original stem is too thick or broken. See pages 68-72.

The shapes of bouquets to consider

Here are the basic shapes which are most commonly used nowadays. The swing of fashion will dictate which shape and size is most popular at any one time – but all are attractive and adaptable. Gone are the huge trails of maidenhair fern which almost hid the bride, so too are the formal sheaves of lilies. Today the 'shower' is the most popular of shapes.

The shape of the bouquet should, however, complement the dress and it should be made an appropriate size for each particular bride.

The suggested shapes are presented to help, but not to restrict your own creativity or that of your florist. Remember that the bouquet is there to please the bride and enhance the day. Beauty is in the eye of the beholder.

SHOWER

WATERFALL

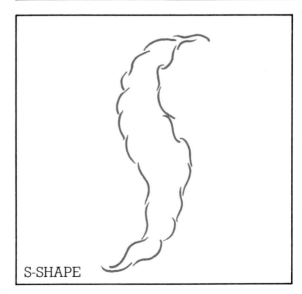

S-SHAPE

VICTORIAN POSY

LOOSE POSY

CRESCENT

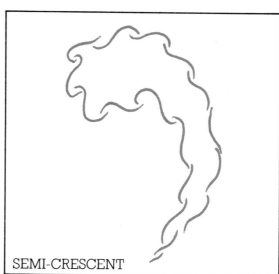

SEMI-CRESCENT

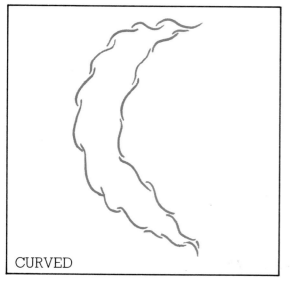

CURVED

STRAIGHT

The technique of wiring

All flowers and foliage for bouquet work and other designs which are to be worn or carried, need to be wired. It is normal to take away most of any stem and replace with a wire which is then covered in stem-wrap. This reduces the weight of the finished bouquet and gives a more delicate appearance. The wire also allows each flower or leaf to be positioned in exactly the right spot and pointed in the right direction.

Different thicknesses (gauges) of wire are available from very fine 'silver' reel wire to chunky stem wires. The general rule is to use the thinnest wire which is just sufficiently strong to do the job required.

Handling fresh flowers is a delicate job and some can bruise easily. You would be well advised to perfect the wiring techniques shown on the following pages using silk material before using fresh flowers.

Single Leg Mount

Use this technique with flowers like carnations or roses which have a solid calyx below the petals.

1. Cut off the flower leaving about 2 inches of stem.

2. Use a stub wire to pierce the calyx and push upwards towards the flower.

3. Twist the wire around the neck and then down the remaining stem.

4. Cover the wire with stem-wrap.

5. Use wire cutters to cut the end to the required length.

Double-Leg Mount

Alternatively, you can use the double-leg mount for an even stronger stem.

1. Cut off the flower leaving about 2 inches of stem.

2. Place the wire across the neck of the bloom.

3. Bend both of the wires parallel to the remaining stem.

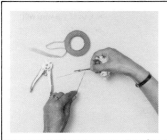

4. Twist the longest wire around the other wire and the stem, working down.

5. Cover the wire with stem-wrap and cut to length.

Feathering

Wiring some of the petals taken from a carnation to produce a small head is called 'feathering'.

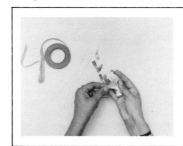

1. Tear off the covering to the calyx.

2. Pull out a small bunch of petals keeping the bases together.

3. Bend a silver wire and place the bend over the petal bases.

4. Twist one of the wire ends (called a 'leg') firmly around the petals and around the other wire. Cut off evenly.

5. Cover the wire with stem-wrap.

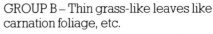

HOW TO WIRE LEAVES

GROUP A – Rose and Ivy leaves, etc.

GROUP B – Thin grass-like leaves like carnation foliage, etc.

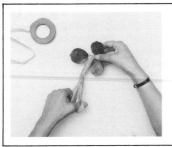

1. Cut off leaf from the stem.

1. Working on the back of the largest leaf, use a long wire to stitch at the base of the leaf.

2. Work on the back of the leaf and stitch a wire through the central vein about two thirds of the way up the leaf.

2. Pull the wire through and stitch again near the tip of the leaf.

3. Pull the wire through to a central position and then draw both ends down parallel.

3. Stitch each side leaf (2 or 4) in the same way leaving about one inch of wire as a stem.

4. Hold the leaf firmly and twist one wire around the remaining stem and the other wire.

4. Gather the leaves together in a fan shape and twist the long stem wire around the others.

5. Cover the wire stem in stem-wrap.

5. Cover the stem with stem-wrap.

Double Leg Mount

Use a stub wire (22 gauge/0.71mm) for large flowers which are going to be used as single blooms or are going to be the main stem of a 'spray'. Use fine silver wire (36 gauge/0.20mm) for small flowers which are subsequently going to be made up into sprays. If you are making up sprays read the section on the next page before you start wiring.

1. Cut off the flower from the stem leaving a small amount of stem attached.

2. Bend a wire and place the bend over the existing stem.

3. Twist one of the wire ends (called a 'leg') firmly around the stem and the other wire.

4. Use wire cutters to cut the ends to the required length.

5. Wrap wires with stem-binding tape.

Making up spray stems

A 'spray' is one stem which carries several individual flowers, normally positioned in a straight line.

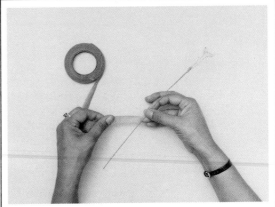

1. Wire the first flower on a 22 gauge (0.71mm) stub wire using a double-leg mount. Stem-wrap from the flower to half-way down the stem.

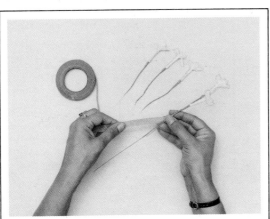

2. In sprays of three or five flowers mount each of the remaining flowers on fine silver rose wire and cover with stem-wrap.

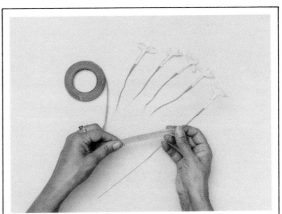

3. Take the first flower on its stub wire and join a roll of stem-wrap some way down the stem.

4. Position the next flower so that it overlaps the first and bind together with stem-wrap. Continue in the same way with the other flowers until a maximum of five flowers are on the stem.

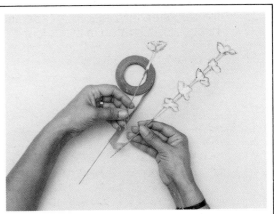

5. If the spray needs to be longer the next flower should be mounted on another 22 gauge (0.71mm) stub wire. Stem-wrap and then bind to the original stem with the roll of tape. By adding extra stub wires like this the spray stem will remain stable.

Before you start

Make sure you have the necessary different gauge wires, tape and binding wire to hand (see Page 6). It is useful to place the different gauges of wire into separate jars as they can very quickly become a tangled mess.

Lay out the flowers and foliage on the table in roughly the required design. Try to determine the amount of flowers you will need and wire all the material you require and cover with stem binding tape. Now make up the required sprays with stem binding tape (see page 72).
You can always wire the odd flower should the need arise; but wires can often be dirty and you will need to wash your hands after wiring so that the flowers remain clean.

When using artificial material do not be tempted to leave some of the flowers with original stems even if they are the required length and thickness. The colour of the stem will almost always vary from that of the stem tape which you are using.

On the following pages you will find detailed instructions on the making of bouquets. Instead of trying to write about the process in vague generalizations we have provided step-by-step instructions for specific bouquets illustrated in the colour section of the book. In this way you can study how each of the different shapes are created and see the back and side view as well.

We hope that with a little practise, especially with wiring, you will be able to make any of the bouquets. The sensible approach is to start with the smaller shapes and to use silk flowers. When you have mastered these, you will soon progress to using fresh flowers and the larger designs.

DESIGN	STEP-BY-STEP INSTRUCTIONS	COLOUR PICTURE
SHOWER	Page 74	Page 19
WATERFALL	Page 77	Page 35
CRESCENT	Page 80	Page 37
STRAIGHT BOUQUET	Page 82	Page 49
LOOSE POSY	Page 84	Page 45
POSY USING FOAM TOPPED HANDLE	Page 86	Page 31
VICTORIAN POSY	Page 87	Page 59
S SHAPE BOUQUET	Use Crescent technique Page 80	
CURVED BOUQUET	Use Straight technique Page 82	
HEAD-DRESS	Page 90	Page 57
POMANDER	Page 88	Page 61
CORSAGE & BUTTONHOLE	Page 91	Page 62
CAKE TOP	Page 79	Page 63

SHOWER BOUQUET

These instructions explain in detail how the shower bouquet on page 19 is made. Use the same principles to make any of the shower bouquets found in the book.

First cut all flowers from the original stems. Wire the five orchids onto individual stub wires using double leg mounts and cover each with stem-wrap tape. Wire all the other material shown in the ingredients list shown on the appropriate shower page (in this case page 18). Make up spray stems at this stage before assembly starts (see page 72 for instructions on making up sprays).

Lay the wired material in front of you in the appropriate groups. A shower bouquet is created in two stages. The first stage is the bottom 2/3rds of the bouquet, so the first stem you use is that which will be carried nearest the ground. The idea is to work from the bottom to the widest point and then from the top to the widest point. You will find it easier to work with your material on this first stage if you hold this as shown in the photograph.

Take a spray stem of Stephanotis (4 flowers) and using a roll of stem-wrap bind in a rose spray of two buds on the left side and another spray of pink larkspur to the right hand side.

Working down, place one spray of pink daisies in the centre of the main stem just below the Stephanotis.

Keep binding down the main stem without crossing any stems and maintain the correct shape. Next tape a spray stem of Lily of the Valley spray to the left of the main stem and 1 Croton leaf to the right. Work in a pink flower spike to left and a pale pink rose bud to the right, keeping the binding neat.

Continue in this way remembering to place the appropriate flower on the top of main stem. As you work down, the centre flowers should be lifted from the stem to avoid a flat appearance. Continue binding in material until the widest point of the bouquet has been reached, generally about 2/3rds of overall length will then have been assembled – detach stem-wrap.

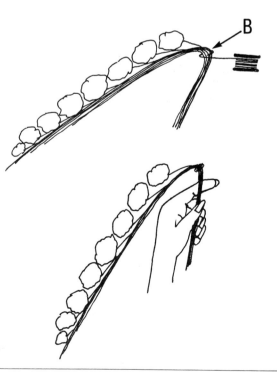

At this stage bend the wire stems back as shown in the illustration.

A reel of silver wire is now required and the end should be attached to the point of the bend in the stem. This can be done by twisting around stem a few times at Point B. From this point on, the binding must continue at the same point. The work from this point is called the 'return end' and you should now hold the bouquet the right way up to complete the work.

Begin this 'return end' with a spray stem of Stephanotis (four flowers) and bind it centrally so that the tip of stem is in the position to create the total length of the bouquet.

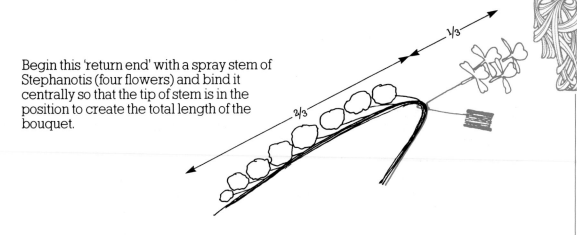

Now place in the outer stems binding in with the silver wire, keeping the binding in the same spot.

The central blooms are placed into the middle in an upright/vertical position, some blooms should be left higher than others. The most important flowers, in this case the orchids, should stand out and be most prominent in the centre of the bouquet. When all the flowers have been bound in cut the remaining wire stems to the correct length to form a handle. Taper this handle as shown on page 94. Make sure it feels comfortable to hold in the hand.

Now twist the silver wire down and around the length of the handle four or five times and pull firmly upwards between the stems before you cut off the wire. The handle is now taped with the stem-wrap. Cover handle with ribbon as shown on Page 94.

WATERFALL BOUQUET

These instructions explain in detail how the waterfall bouquet pictured on page 35 is made. On page 34 you will find a list of the ingredients used. The same principles can be used to make any other waterfall bouquets.

Arrange flowers roughly into the design required, by laying them on a table making sure you have the right length of stems to form the cascade effect of this design. The starting point for the binding of a waterfall bouquet is much closer to the centre point when compared with a conventional shower bouquet. It is therefore necessary to use more than one stub wire with some of the longest sprays to achieve the length of stem required.

Begin by binding together with stem-wrap the longest 7 leaf Ivy spray with the longest Stephanotis spray and a spray containing 2 spikes of Lily of the Valley. Have the material facing you with the flowers pointing up. The overall length will be about 14″.

With a waterfall design, all the material flows from a single binding point. Now add a 5 leaf Ivy spray, a long stem of Lily of the Valley and then a long spray of lilies. The Lilies are positioned above the first central ivy spray. Add other material on both sides, not moving the binding point by more than an inch.

Place three of the rose stems and leaves at appropriate intervals until the widest point of the bouquet has been reached. About two thirds of the overall bouquet length will now have been completed.

Detach the stem-wrap and bend the stems down and under so that you can begin the return end. Attach silver wire to the point of the bend.

Hold the face of the bouquet away you with the first part pointing to the ground. Bind at this point a spray stem of five Stephanotis flowers to give the total length of the bouquet. This is the first placement of the return end.

Continue placing material on both sides of the stephanotis, beginning at the top and working toward the centre forming the outline as you go.

Finally bind in the central material, making sure the central rose is placed in vertically.

When finished, cut and taper the stems to form a handle. Twist the silver wire around and down the handle three or four times and pull the wire up sharply between the stems to secure. Cut off the wire, wrap the handle with stem-wrap and then cover with ribbon. Fix a bow at the top of the handle just by the binding point (See Page 94).

CAKE TOP

The colours used for your cake top should be the same shade as those used in the bride's bouquet. The vase is normally silver or white, unless you have been asked to use an object of sentimental value to the bride. Select small flowers for the cake top so that the arrangement is light and dainty. This attractive cake top is illustrated in colour on page 63.

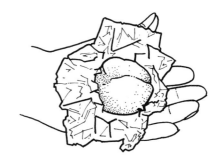

To begin, cut the flowers from the original stems leaving about ½" (1 cm) of stem below each bloom. Wire the flowers with a double leg mount, cover the wire with stem-wrap and make up sprays as listed.

Take a piece of Dri-hard, wrap in aluminium foil and place into the vase. The first flower in position is the central gypsophila cut to length. Remember that the tip of this flower dictates the overall height of the arrangement.

Next place the five ivy sprays around the edge of the vase, bending the sprays downward. Then place the four Gypsophila stems between the Ivy, again bending the stems down.

Lily of the Valley sprays are placed in above the gypsophila, about 1" (2 cm) shorter. Gradually fill in with the rest of the material until all the gaps are filled. If ribbon trails are required, place these around the bottom edge and cut to length.

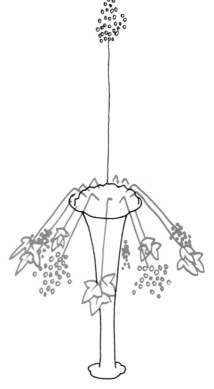

CRESCENT

For this example we given details of how the Full Crescent shown on page 37 was created. With all crescents choose several shades of colour and if possible different flowers. If using say two types of flowers i.e. Roses and Lilies use varying sizes and shades. Foliage may also be used if required.

Cut all material from the original stems, wire and stem-wrap each piece (see pages 68-73). Make up into sprays the material indicated on the ingredients page. This bouquet is worked in two halves. Therefore make sure that the material is separated into two equal amounts before assembly.

To start the first half take the longest spray and curve to the right (facing you) add the second longest spray to the left of first spray, binding with stem-wrap, so that the top flower is approximately 1½ inches (4 cm) from the top of first spray.

Add two more sprays in this way on the same side, then add a spray on the right side of the main group, curving the work as you go.

Now establish the curve outline by adding sprays until centre top of bouquet is reached.

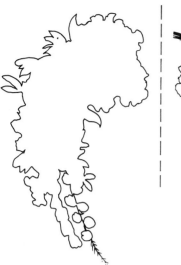

It would be useful at this stage to stand in front of a mirror to check if this half of the bouquet is the required shape and size.

Place the first half of the crescent bouquet in front of you and start to make up the second half of the bouquet exactly the same as the first but curving in the opposite direction. As you go along, keep checking that the outline shape and position of the flowers are identical.

When you have finished, check in front of the mirror holding both halves together in the required position.

Bend the handles of both sprays down and join together with silver reel wire using 34 gauge (0.24mm) or thicker. Keep the binding at one spot. Now add the material to make the centre of the crescent, the ribbon bows are also placed in at this stage, still binding in one spot.

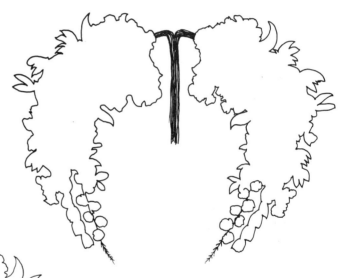

To finish off, wind the wire down the stem and pull firmly up between the wire stems. Taper the handle by cutting out some wires and the wrap with stem-wrap. Cover the handle with ribbon and place bow on handle as per instructions on page 94.

◫ S-Shaped bouquets

These bouquets are made in the same way – two halves joined together and then filled in with the central flowers. The differences are that to make an S-shape the bottom section is larger than the top and the direction of curves when made are the same.

— 81 —

STRAIGHT BOUQUET

These instructions explain in detail how the straight bouquet on page 49 is made. Use the same principles to make any of the straight bouquets found in the book.

Cut all material from original stems. The Nephrolepis leaves are mounted onto 14″ (35 cm) long stub wire and covered with stem-wrap – carnations and blossom are mounted on 12″ (30 cm) long stub wire. Make sprays with other material as per the ingredient list on page 48 and make bows.

Begin with the longest Nephrolepis leaf, and with work facing you, place the second longest leaf to the right and bind in with stem-wrap. Bind in the longest larkspur stem to the left.

Now bind in the double tail ribbon. A spray of three azaleas is bound in on top of the main leaf so that the top flower of this spray starts well down the leaf.

Next place larkspur blossom to the left of the main stem and a short leaf to the right. A double loop ribbon is next positioned slightly to the left falling over the blossom.

The central material which is bound in next should be lifted slightly from their stems so that the faces of the flowers are seen.

Add in material in this way until about three quarters of the overall length has been reached, and two carnations have been added.

Now detach stem-wrap and bend wires down and under so that you can work on the return end. Attach silver wire at the bend.

Turn the face of the bouquet away from you and start the return end with the longest Nephrolepis leaf positioned to the left of centre. Keep the binding to one point and place the two remaining leaves and outline material.

Finally fill in the centre with the large full bow and the remaining carnation.

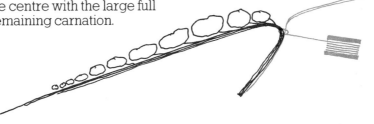

Check the face of the bouquet and adjust the position of the leaves so that they follow a line from right top to bottom left. The blossom flowers should mirror this line on the opposite side (top left to bottom right).

Taper the stems and trim to form a comfortable size handle. Twist the wire around and down a few times and firmly pull upwards between the stems to secure. Cut off the wire and bind the handle with stem-wrap. Cover with ribbon and add a bow as shown on page 94.

Curved bouquets

These bouquets are made in the same way apart from curving the stems as the work progresses.

LOOSE POSY

The large loose posy shown on page 45 is an attractive alternative to the more formal and regimented design of a Victorian posy. Note that the flowers do NOT make circles around a central point.

Remove all material from the original stems, wire, stem-wrap and make flowers into sprays where necessary. If larger material is used such as roses or freesias mount singly onto stub wires.

For the outline, equal numbers of leaves and flowers are required. Sprays of 3 rose leaves can be used, or if small leaves are used, such as Ivy leaves, then make sprays of 3 or 5 leaves using the stitch method as explained on Page 70.

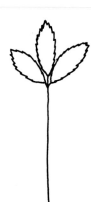

If a small to medium posy is required use 6 leaves and 6 flowers for the outline. For the large posy illustrated on page 45, you will need 8 stems of each. Split them into two equal groups face upwards. Place the two groups face to face, keeping the points together – Bind with silver wire at the required point keeping the binding in one spot. The lower the binding point the larger the posy. If a small size is required, make the binding point higher.

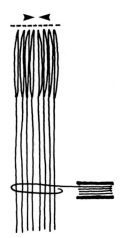

With the work facing you, bend down the lower four leaves evenly spaced and then arrange the upper four leaves to make a circular outline with equal spaces between each leaf.

Position sprays of flowers between leaves, wiring in at the same point. The outline is now complete.

Keep binding in one spot and place in the other flowers, working from the outside towards the centre. Some sprays of short foliage can be worked into the back if the posy seems a little thin.

Taper the wires so that the handle is of a comfortable thickness as shown on page 94. Twist silver wire down the stem and pull up through the wire stems and cut off.

Stem-wrap the handle and cover with ribbon. Place a bow at the top of the handle as shown on Page 94.

POSY USING
FOAM-TOPPED HANDLE

The use of a ready-made posy base, complete with handle and foam top makes arranging very easy, and success guaranteed. Try to use different shades of colour in the flowers to add interest. These instructions will explain how the posy shown on page 31 was made.

All material is removed from original stems and wired and stem-wrapped on individual wires. Small flowers are made into sprays while larger blooms are mounted singly.

Make double loop ribbon bows (see page 93), on wires using a shade of ribbon that blends in with the flowers used.

First slip the chosen frill onto the handle to give the overall dimensions of the finished posy. Many frills need to be trimmed with scissors to make a scallop edge. Now position the foliage around the outside edge of the frill, leaving some of the net showing.

Place flowers between leaves alternating shade and variety.

Place centre flower at top, this should be one of the important flowers. Work down and fill in the posy with flowers and bows.

Ensure the frill is tight up to the foliage and secure with pins. To finish off, a bow can be placed at the top of the handle under the frill or it can be left plain.

VICTORIAN POSY

The Victorian Posy is generally made up of neat, circular bands of flowers arranged around a central bloom. The one explained here is shown at the bottom of page 59. This type of posy is normally carried by small bridesmaids, but there are no hard and fast rules.

Begin by cutting the stems down to about ¾″ (2 cm) and double-leg mount each flower with a stub wire and stem-wrap each one. Holding the central rose in one hand add the first circlet of flowers, one at a time binding in with reel wire. Make sure the central flower is slightly higher than the surrounding blooms.

For the next circle use slightly larger flowers and position them slightly lower than the first circlet.

Make up several single loops of ribbon and wire each one as shown on page 92. Bind these ribbons into the posy, making sure the trail of ribbon is the required length.

Continue using this method until the required size has been reached.

Secure the reel wire by going down the handle and then back up again. Taper the handle as shown on page 94 and then bind the handle with stem-wrap. Slip the doily over the handle and secure with a Pearl Headed pin.

POMANDER

These instructions explain in detail how the pomander shown on page 61 is made. Using the same principle of quarter sections you can make any variety of pomander. Ensure the ribbon is fixed firmly, some bridesmaids will swing your delicate pomander around like a weapon of war.

Fold a length of ribbon in half to the required length of handle. If a very small child is to carry the pomander make the ribbon handle short. Fix the cut ends of ribbon with a double leg mount, using a long stub wire. Make sure the wiring is tight and firm.

Push wire ends into a foam ball until both ends protrude and the ribbon is close to the foam. Then bend the wires and push the ends back into the ball, making sure that the ribbon is secure and cannot come out when being held.

Cut all the flower material and foliage from the original stems and wire each with a double leg mount as detailed on pages 68-71. Tape with stem-wrap. Make double loop ribbon bows (see page 93) using double leg mounts in the same way as the flowers and foliage have been wired and stem-wrapped.

The Gypsophila used in the pomander shown on page 61 is generally bought on large stems with many blooms on each stem. In this pomander we have used two small pieces bound together to make a spray. Start by inserting alternate flowers, foliage and bows making a circle all around the outer edge working from top to bottom.

Then repeat down the centre at front and again at the back leaving four quarters to be filled.

Now fill in each quarter, remembering to alternate the material until a well balanced flower ball has been created, making sure that all gaps have been filled.

Now make four double loop ribbon bows using a double leg mount for each and bind with stem-wrap. Push these into the top of the ball around the ribbon handle.

If ribbon ends are required at top of handle this can be accomplished by simply tying a length of ribbon leaving the required lengths.

FULL HEAD-DRESS

These instructions explain in detail how the full peach coronet shown on page 57 was made. Use the same principles to make any head-dress.

Cover the three stub wires with stem-wrap. After removing flowers from their original stems, mount each flower on silver wire using a double leg mount, bind with stem-wrap and then cut wires to approximately 1½" (4 cm) long.

Take the first stub wire and attach the first Lily of the Valley flower with stem-wrap, starting 3" (8 cm) down the wire and placing it to the left of the wire.

Next bind in to the right another Lily of the Valley, then attach alternate dianthus and stephanotis down the centre. Add a rose and Lily of the Valley as in the diagram.

All flowers should be attached in the same order all the way round, but the direction in which each flower points should change a little so that straight lines are avoided.

Work down the first stub wire until about 2" (5 cm) are left bare, then attach the second wire by laying the top of the new wire beside the last 1½" (4 cm) of the first wire and bind together with stem-wrap.

Carry on adding flowers in the same way, until the third stub wire is added. The size obviously depends on the size of the bride's head and where on the head it is to be worn. When the required length has been achieved, make sure the last flower does not match the first. Measure 2" (5 cm) past the last flower and cut off the remaining wire. Bend round into shape and twist spare wires around the main stem, carefully positioning between the flowers.

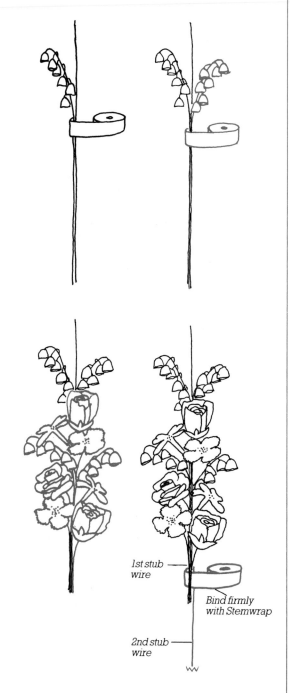

1st stub wire

Bind firmly with Stemwrap

2nd stub wire

MAKING CORSAGES

These instructions are specific to the bright orchid corsage shown on page 62.

Ingredients
Fern Leaves
4 stems × 1 leaf
Orchids
4 stems × 1 flower

Begin by wiring each piece and covering the mechanics with stem-wrap. Place the first orchid on top of the first leaf with the material facing you and bind stems together with stem-wrap.

The second orchid is placed to the left of the top orchid, but lower. Now bind in the next two fern leaves as shown.
After the third orchid is bound in, the return end position has been reached. Tear off the stem wrap and bend the wires to form a miniature handle.

Attach the silver reel wire on the bend and bind in the last fern giving the over-all length. Now place in the last orchid keeping the wire binding in the same place.

Twist the wire down and up the stem to secure it and then detach wire. Trim ends of wire, taper if necessary and then stem-wrap.

MAKING BUTTONHOLES

A buttonhole is usually one carnation or rose wired with its own or asparagus foliage.

Prepare fresh flowers by wiring as shown on page 68. With silk flowers use the alternative double leg mount.

If using asparagus foliage tape the stem, but do not wire. Other foliage should be wired as shown on page 70.

To make up the buttonhole simply place the flower onto the foliage and bind together with stem-wrap.

TYING RIBBONS

Many people find that tying ribbons and bows to make them look pretty is a difficult job. However with a little practice and the following step-by-step instructions everyone should be able to add a crisp bow to their arrangements without trouble.

Tail

This ribbon piece is simply a length of ribbon which has been pinched together at one end with a double leg wire added.

1. Bend a stub wire in half.

2. Pinch the end 1 inch of ribbon together and place the bend of wire onto the ribbon.

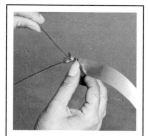

3. Twist one wire leg around the ribbon and the other wire to firmly trap the ribbon and produce a sturdy stem.

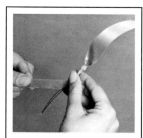

4. Use wire cutters to trim ends evenly. Wrap wires with stem-binding tape.

Single Loop

This is the most versatile of ribbon pieces. It can be used singly or can be positioned with stems pointing towards each other to give the impression of a figure of eight bow.

1. Hold the ribbon to make one loop and a tail to the required length.

2. Pinch the end of the loop firmly together and hold. Then cut the remaining ribbon from the roll.

3. Bend a stub wire in half and place the bend over the pinched end of the ribbon.

4. Twist as tightly as possible and wire leg around the pinched part of the ribbon and the other length of wire.

5. Twist several times to trap the ribbon and produce a sturdy stem.

6. Cut wires to required length.

7. Wrap wires with stem-binding tape.

8. Pull the loop into shape.

Double Loop

A useful ribbon piece for the experienced arranger.

1. Hold the ribbon to make two loops and a tail to the required length.

2. Follow steps 2-8 as shown in the Single Loop instructions.

Triple Loop

For bigger and bold arrangements this larger bow is most useful.

1. Hold the ribbon to make three loops and a tail to the required length.

2. Follow steps 2-8 as shown in the Single Loop instructions.

Figure of Eight Bow

Illustrated below is the easiest way for the inexperienced to tie a figure of eight bow. A professional will pinch the ribbon together at each stage, but this needs practice.

1. Fold the ribbon to the required size so that you have three layers.

2. Cut off the remaining ribbon.

3. Pinch the centre of the ribbon together tightly.

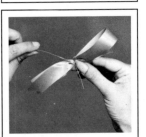

4. Twist a fine silver wire firmly around the pinched ribbon.

5. Twist one wire leg around the other a couple of times.

6. Pull the loops into shape.

MAKING HANDLES AND
COVERING IN RIBBON

1. After binding in the final flower of the bouquet, bind with reel wire firmly and securely several times round.

2. Taper the wires to thin out the over-all width of the handle by cutting out some of the ends of the stub wires.

3. Trim the remaining wires to form the end of the handle.

4. Twist the wire round the handle, down to within ½″ (1 cm) from the end.

5. Pull the wire firmly up through the middle of the wires, and then bind around several times going round the handle. Cut off the wire.

6. Cover the handle with stem-wrap working from the top to the end.

7. Cut off about 4 ft (120 cm) of narrow ribbon and position at the top of the handle. There should be ⅔rds of the ribbon on one side of the handle and the other ⅓rd on the other side. Take the longest piece and start winding around and down the handle, pulling tightly.

8. At the end of the handle fold over the ribbon and insert a pearl topped pin.

9. Wind the ribbon up the handle firmly and at the top secure with another pin.

10. Make a figure of eight bow with a separate piece of ribbon (See page 93).

11. Use the two ends of ribbon to attach the bow to the handle. Trim ribbon ends to the required length.

INDEX

Anchors 7
Apricot Pomander 61
Apricot Waterfall 34

Basket 60
Blue & White Semi-Crescent 16
Buttonholes 62

Cake Top Illustrated 63, 64
Cake Top Making 79
Corsages Illustrated 62
Corsage Making 91
Crescent Bouquet Illustrated 15, 37
Crescent Bouquet Making 80-81
Curved Bouquet Making 83

Double Leg Mount 69, 71
Double Loop Bow 93
Dri-Hard 7

Equipment 6

Feathering 69
Figure of Eight Bow 93
Flower types 5
Foam 7
Foam-Topped Handle 7, 86
Freesias & Pink Roses 54

Glossary 65

Handle Making 94-95
Head-dresses Illustrated 57
Head-dress Making 90

Large Lemon Orchids 32
Lemon & Green 48
Lemon & Pink Loose Posy 44
Lemon & White S 20
Lemon Lilies 10
Lemon Posy 30
Light & Dark Pink Shower 46
Loose Posy Illustrated 31, 45, 53, 59
Loose Posy Making 84-85

Materials 4

Oasis fix 7
Open Peach Posy 52

Peach Cascade 28
Peach Lilies & Net 38
Peach Pigtails 42
Peach Roses 22

Peaches & Cream Straight Bouquet 28
Pearl Posy 58
Pink & Lemon Handspray 24
Pink Orchids & Roses 18
Pins 6
Pomander Illustrated 61
Pomander Making 88-89
Posy Frills 7
Posy Making Using Foam Topped Handle 86
Pink Basket 60
Prayer Book Design 56

Red & White Crescent 14
Red Roses 50
Return End 76
Ribbon Bows 92-93
Ribbon Handles 94-95
Ring Pillow 56

S Shaped Bouquet Illustrated 21
S Shaped Bouquet Making 81
Scissors 6
Semi-Crescent Bouquet 17, 39
Shades of Lavender 36
Shades of Pink 12
Shapes of Bouquets 66-67
Shower Bouquet Illustrated 9, 11, 13, 19, 23, 25, 33, 41, 43, 47, 51, 55
Shower Bouquet Making 74-76
Single Leg Mount 68
Single Loop Bow 92
Spray Stems 72
Spraying Up 72
Stay Soft 7
Stem-wrap 6
Straight Bouquet Illustrated 29, 49
Straight Bouquet Making 82-83

Tape 6
Tapering Handles 94
Triple Loop Bow 93

Victorian Posy Illustrated 58
Victorian Posy Making 87

Waterfall Bouquet Illustrated 35
Waterfall Bouquet Making 77-78
White & Lemon Shower 40
White Lace Shower 8
Wire cutters 6
Wires 6
Wiring Flowers 68, 69, 71
Wiring Leaves 70